# What's It Al' Armoured

## The Christian Has Spiritual Armour

# What's It All About, Alphy?
# Armoured For The Fight

## The Christian Has Spiritual Armour

### Davo Roberts

PULP theology

Books written to help you. Clearly.

www.pulptheology.com
www.pulptheology.co.uk

# Acknowledgements

What's It All About, Alphy? Armoured For The Fight – version 1.0

Book 4 in the "What's It All About, Alphy?" Series

Also available in full colour on Kindle

Text & Graphics Copyright © 2022 Dave G Roberts

ISBN: 9798359918879

This has previously been released as Podcasts on the Partakers website: www.partakers.co.uk

This chapter previously released in text format in PulpTheology book "Engaged In Battle"

# Dedication

*Firstly, to the Lord our God – Father, Son and Holy Spirit. I wouldn't be here without him.*

Secondly to my wife, Youngmi. She is my one and only partner. I can't imagine life without her. I thank God for her daily.

*Roger Kirby, who was mentor, editor, but most of all good friend. He fought the good fight and is now in the presence of His saviour, Jesus Christ.*

# How To Look Up The Bible

Book of the Bible. In this case, the book of Luke. Don't be afraid to look at the contents page to find it. We all do it, even if we don't want to admit it!

This is the Verse of the Chapter. In this case, it is verse 9. Think of it as a sentence or part of a sentence.

This is the chapter of the book. In this case, Chapter 19.

# Contents

# Introduction: Armour Engaged

¹⁰ Finally, be strong in the Lord and in his mighty power. ¹¹ Put on the full armour of God, so that you can take your stand against the devil's schemes. ¹² For our struggle is not against flesh and blood, but against the rulers, against the authorities, against the powers of this dark world and against the spiritual forces of evil in the heavenly realms.

¹³ Therefore put on the full armour of God, so that when the day of evil comes, you may be able to stand your ground, and after you have done everything, to stand. ¹⁴ Stand firm then, with the belt of truth buckled round your waist, with the breastplate of righteousness in place, ¹⁵ and with your feet fitted with the readiness that comes from the gospel of peace.

¹⁶ In addition to all this, take up the shield of faith, with which you can extinguish all the flaming arrows of the evil one. ¹⁷ Take the helmet of salvation and the sword of the Spirit, which is the word of God.
(Ephesians 6v10–17)

As Christians, those who are following Jesus Christ, there is usually a great pressure to compromise our life of faith whereby we are pressured to be disobedient to God.

We get those insatiable thoughts of lust, revenge or pride.
Doubts set in. Guilt appears constant.

This pressure comes from our adversaries: Satan, the world and our old sinful nature.

To help us in this fight, God has designed spiritual armour to be worn during this battle.

¹⁵ Truth is nowhere to be found,
and whoever shuns evil becomes a prey.
The LORD looked and was displeased
that there was no justice.
¹⁶ He saw that there was no one,
he was appalled that there was no one to
intervene;
so his own arm achieved salvation for him,
and his own righteousness sustained him.
¹⁷ He put on righteousness as his breastplate,
and the helmet of salvation on his head;
he put on the garments of vengeance
and wrapped himself in zeal as in a cloak.
(Isaiah 59v15-17)

This armour is what God wears when He goes out to battle.

What are the hallmarks of this spiritual armour we are to wear?

**The Bible**

This is our attack weapon. That is why we are to study it and learn from it, trusting in the Holy Spirit who lives with us to lead and reveal it to us.

We are to grow in grace and in the knowledge of Jesus, says Peter (2 Peter 3v18).

This is achieved only through our spending time studying the Bible and seeing what God has to say to us.

When we hear those nagging little voices that say to us "God didn't say that!", we can reply most emphatically "Oh yes, He most certainly did!"

**Faith**

We are to show total trust in God for every aspect of our life.

The faith we have is a defensive weapon against the mistruths that come into our head.

Mistruths such as lies, blasphemy, lust, greed, selfishness are all little darts thrown at us by satan and others.

By maintaining our trust in God's promises and God's power, these little darts are extinguished.

Righteousness

As Christians, we are to live a life which is totally honouring to God and bringing Him glory to God by letting truth permeate every facet of our life.

When we started out being a Christian, before Almighty God Himself, we were given the righteousness of Jesus.

But that righteousness needs to be lived out in our life as a Christian. If it isn't, then we can be assured that satan will attack and accuse us incessantly.

Another question now. How do we put this armour on?

Well, it is not through some mystical, deep and secret process! If it were, then we probably wouldn't wear it.

The armour is revealed, whenever we resist the works of satan, and ignore the lies he tells us.

For example, when our love for others reflects the sacrificial love that Jesus showed, our spiritual armour is displayed.

# 1. Belt of Truth

¹ Dear friends, do not believe every spirit, but test the spirits to see whether they are from God, because many false prophets have gone out into the world.
² This is how you can recognise the Spirit of God: every spirit that acknowledges that Jesus Christ has come in the flesh is from God, ³ but every spirit that does not acknowledge Jesus is not from God. This is the spirit of the antichrist, which you have heard is coming and even now is already in the world.
(1 John 4v1-3)

Truth is the belt which holds all other items of the armour in place. Today we hear constantly that there are no absolute truths anymore.

People and society say to us: "What is true for us may not be true for you. What is true for you may not be true for me."

What, therefore, is truth? The idea of truth in the Old Testament was used in two ways.

Firstly, facts may be either true or false – an intellectual truth. An example would be that Moses existed as a person. That is a fact. It is therefore self-evidently true.

Truth can also be used to define a characteristic of a reliable person, such as the test of Joseph's brothers (Genesis 42:16). These truths are also used to describe God as a true God, rather than the pagan gods belonging to the nations around Israel.

Truth, or being true, is described as a characteristic of Yahweh, the God of Israel. He is consistently true and therefore is undeniably trustworthy in all His ways. God's loving care is trustworthy and is seen throughout His dealings with Israel.

In the New Testament, Christianity itself is seen as truth (Galatians 2:5; Ephesians 1:13). Indeed, Jesus, the head of the Church, said that He was the only truth, the only life and the only way to God (John 14:6).

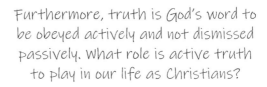

Furthermore, truth is God's word to be obeyed actively and not dismissed passively. What role is active truth to play in our life as Christians?

Having and possessing a growing knowledge of biblical truth enables our character to develop, building our spiritual strength and maturity.

Since understanding the Bible increases our knowledge of God, it also increases the possibilities for us to reveal to others, our transformation by Jesus.

This is a transformation where we are seen to love, grow and serve.

However, for truth to be effective, it needs to be a truth with life in it. That is where we will be an active doer of the Bible's suggestions and commands and not merely a passive hearer.

Our life as Christians is to be a balance of love and truth. They must coexist with each other in our thinking.

Then through that knowledge, service and faith in Almighty God, we will continually grow and be strengthened in all aspects of our life.

All to God's praise, glory and honour alone. As we wear the belt of truth, we will be growing more like Jesus Christ in every aspect of our daily life.

Growing more like Jesus is a lifelong process. In the words of the Bible, it is one of the big words – sanctification. 'Sanctify' is one of the words used in English to translate a connected set of Hebrew or Greek words. Other words include holy, saintly, and consecrate. A rather mixed lot.

Looking at them all together gives a good idea what they all mean. They are all to do with the long and difficult process by which an ordinary person, like us, gets to be more like Jesus.

If we, as disciples of Jesus Christ, are showing the fruit of the Spirit, then we are becoming Christ-like and we are being sanctified.

Sometimes that growth as Christians is a difficult path for us, but nobody said that it would be easy. Certainly, Jesus never said that it would be.

Another way to look at growing or sanctification, is that it is like the changing of a caterpillar into a butterfly – it's a process. As we grow more like Jesus Christ, this gives people a reason to ask why we seem to be so different.

This process of sanctification affects every aspect of our life as we mature in Jesus Christ, for we are being transformed and becoming more like Him.

"And we know that in all things God works for the good of those who love Him, who have been called according to His purpose. For those God foreknew He also predestined to be conformed to the likeness of His Son, that He might be the firstborn among many brothers and sisters."
(Romans 8:28-29)

'And we all, who with unveiled faces contemplate the Lord's glory, are being transformed into His image with ever-increasing glory, which comes from the Lord, who is the Spirit.' (2 Corinthians 3:18)

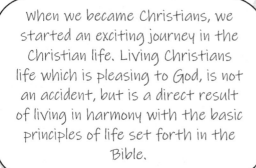

When we became Christians, we started an exciting journey in the Christian life. Living Christians life which is pleasing to God, is not an accident, but is a direct result of living in harmony with the basic principles of life set forth in the Bible.

We are aware that the Christian life is not a matter of expecting spiritual maturity to occur overnight.

16 All Scripture is God-breathed and is useful for teaching, rebuking, correcting and training in righteousness, 17 so that the servant of God may be thoroughly equipped for every good work.
(2 Timothy 3:16–17)

The Bible lays down standards and principles of living. Through reading and studying the Bible, we learn what God expects of us and what guidelines He has given us to achieve this quality of life.

As we apply the principles and guidelines of the Bible to our life, we are continually transformed into the likeness of Christ. Which is the journey we are on. A happy and good life is possible. Jesus, the Lord and Master of all Christians, said: "I have come that they may have life, and have it to the full." (John 10:10)

This is achieved as we allow Jesus Christ to live this life through us so that we start to think and respond like He would do, to the people and circumstances around us.

We continue to learn how to see circumstances and people from God's perspective, rather than reacting on the basis of our own feelings and perspective.
When we respond to circumstances on the basis of our feelings that is when conflict, stress, tension and depression confront us.

When we respond to people and circumstances by looking from God's perspective, we build and reveal a transformed character. We become spiritually mature and live a life which is being transformed into the image of Jesus Christ and worthy of His name.

This is done by remembering to do it in the power of the Holy Spirit living within us. Living in our own strength may get some limited success, but if we rely on the power of the Holy Spirit, we will live a whole life that is worthy of Jesus Christ.

We wear the belt of truth.

# 2. Breastplate of Righteousness

[18] 'If the world hates you, keep in mind that it hated me first. [19] If you belonged to the world, it would love you as its own. As it is, you do not belong to the world, but I have chosen you out of the world. That is why the world hates you. [20] Remember what I told you: "A servant is not greater than His master." If they persecuted me, they will persecute you also. If they obeyed my teaching, they will obey yours also. [21] They will treat you this way because of my name, for they do not know the one who sent me. [22] If I had not come and spoken to them, they would not be guilty of sin; but now they have no excuse for their sin. [23] Whoever hates me hates my Father as well. [24] If I had not done among them the works no one else did, they would not be guilty of sin. As it is, they have seen, and yet they have hated both me and my Father. [25] But this is to fulfil what is written in their Law: "They hated me without reason." [26] 'When the Advocate comes, whom I will send to you from the Father – the Spirit of truth who goes out from the Father – He will testify about me. [27] And you also must testify, for you have been with me from the beginning.

(John 15v18–27)

As Christians, we have a new identity and because of this, we are to stay faithful to Jesus and His will for us, regardless of all opposition and alternatives. What is more, there is help at hand for us to grasp, because the Holy Spirit lives within us as Comforter and Counsellor.

By allowing Him to do this, we are standing alone and being faithful to Him. That is showing the righteousness of Jesus which has been bestowed upon us, because we are born again and Christians.

Satan brings pressure to bear on us as Christians to reduce our standards and our commitment to Jesus Christ. being sanctified.

We undergo challenges from Satan and from those that don't like or understand us and who are constantly tempting us to do wrong things or not to do right things.

Consequently, we are to be separate from sin but not separated from the sinful society where we live, work and recreate.

The key to this standing alone is that we are to have a constant identification with Jesus Christ in every aspect of our life including our thought life, attitudes, actions and in the words that we speak.

Satan brings pressure to bear on us as Christians to reduce our standards and our commitment to Jesus Christ. being sanctified.

However, as we live out our Christian life, we know that there are hindrances to identifying with Jesus.

Here are just three major areas that as Christians, we have to struggle through. Firstly, there is the fear of losing friends. To have the right friends of course, a person must be willing to have enemies.

Jesus made friends on the basis of who would accept Him and His message. We may indeed be excluded from the company of those who reject Jesus (Luke 6:26).

Secondly, there is the insatiable desire to be like those who are not Christians.

Then finally, there is an inborn fear of our worrying what other people will think. This is a fear of being different and being scornfully laughed at.

Therefore, if those are some of the hindrances, what are some of the keys in our overcoming these hindrances? We are to remember God's way of life is superior and leads to a fulfilled life, according to Jesus (John 10:10–11)

As we Christians act as light and salt in the world, with the help of the Holy Spirit within us and empowering us, we will be co-operating with God and He will be being honoured and glorified (1 Peter 4:12–14).

If we give people no reason to ask about the hope and faith that we have in Jesus, they probably won't ask us.

As Christians, we shouldn't apologize for what we know and believe to be a superior way of life. We should never apologise for engaging in the work of evangelism. However, that does not mean we should be arrogant about it because we are also commanded to walk with humility.

We are to just be natural about it. We are to let our spiritual life be natural and our natural life be spiritual. One way to do this, is for us to hold onto the idea that we are not our own boss.

We are to let Jesus take both the strain and glory. Those who reject us, are ultimately also rejecting Jesus.

How can we make the right decisions in questionable areas?

When we are in a difficult situation and we have to make a correct decision in a questionable area, we can ask ourselves questions such as: "Does it bring glory to God?" "Can I truly thank God for this activity?"

Indeed, we ask ourselves, "Could Jesus accompany us in it? "Does this help to build a transformed Christian character?" "Will this cause another Christian to sin/stumble?"

We know beyond doubt, and have assurance, that we can rely on the Holy Spirit who lives with us, to help us, asking for His help and guidance.

We know beyond doubt, and have assurance that we can rely on the Holy Spirit to help us, asking for His help and guidance. If in doubt, we can forget the question or simply wait until the right time.

We know beyond doubt, and have assurance that we can rely on the Holy Spirit to help us, asking for His help and guidance. If in doubt, we can forget the question or simply wait until the right time (Romans 14:22-23). We can also ask other Christians, for advice.

Overall, we are to abstain from all appearances of evil (1 Thessalonians 5:22). Then as we do this, our worldview is being constantly changed and transformed.

A worldview is the way we see the world in which we live, particularly what we think of how other people think and why they act the way they do. The part we are interested in, is that part of how we think about God and our relationship to Him.

The prevalent view, particularly in the West, is exhibited by following what is commonly called the "Golden Rule ", which is "to do to others, what you would have them do to you." Furthermore, they say that there are no certainties or absolutes in life, simply your own individual perspective.

This view says that 'morality is a private thing and what is right for you, may not be right for us and don't you dare tell us that we are wrong in any aspect of our life, because our morals are mine and mine alone, and that is our right.'

As for religion, this prevalent worldview suggests that all religions inevitably lead to some form of god or gods – that is if any god exists at all.
This is seen in the prevalent view particularly in the West, which is that of Darwinism and Scientific Humanism.

Humanists and atheists argue that human beings are merely a miniscule section in nature's rich spectrum, and that Darwinism explains not only how humans got here but that the purpose of humanity has evolved unrestrained biologically and sexually.

This worldview sees no reason for a creator or any form of intelligent designer, as humanity merely evolved by pure chance and random variations.
Further to this, humanity is seen as nothing more than just one little twig, or cell, amongst the order of primates.

All the while, admitting that humankind has probably evolved as far as they can and that there is no definitely accepted account of how life first began. This atheistic and naturalistic theory goes on to deny the very existence of a spiritual world and claims that emotions such as love, fear, hatred and guilt, and thoughts and feelings, are merely physical or chemical in origin.

Contrast these with Christians worldview. Humanistic views are entirely theoretical and are based entirely upon a basic presupposition that there cannot be any form of deity, whether personal or impersonal, and belief that any kind of faith is blind, non-evidential and irrational.

Contrast those worldviews with Christians worldview which states that humanity, both male and female, is made in the image of God and reflects God.

When God created humanity, it was in His own image that all humans were created.

As Christians, we believe therefore, that the whole person, regardless of who they are or what they have done or will do, is valuable to God, and not just the spirit (1 Thessalonians 5:23).

God created humanity, in His own image therefore higher than the animal world. Humanity subsequently rebelled and disobeyed God. God then took the initiative and promised a way out through His chosen Messiah, who we know as Jesus Christ.

Jesus Christ was simultaneously had both divine and human natures.
It was He, who as God, stepped into history and became confined for a short while by time and

He was born so that when He died on the cross, it was to pay the price so that all of humanity could be freed from slavery to sin and disobedience. How so?

If they only chose to accept and believe in Him as God. He rose again physically from the dead, ascended into heaven and now sits at the right hand of the Father. Those who don't accept Him as Lord and Saviour will spend eternity apart from Him.

Jesus Christ is the only way to God, and all other paths lead to ultimate destruction, despite the whispers and lies of Satan.
That is why Christianity is the only true and permanent hope for the world.

As Christians, living in the 21st century, we are to place God first, others second and our own self last. That is the path that we as Christians are to walk, as we follow God alone and serving both Him and other people. As we do this, the worldview we maintain, sees that we will continue being transformed into the very image of Jesus Christ (Philippians 3:20–21).

We put on the breastplate of righteousness.

# 3. Gospel Feet

[1] And so it was with me, brothers and sisters. When I came to you, I did not come with eloquence or human wisdom as I proclaimed to you the testimony about God. [2] For I resolved to know nothing while I was with you except Jesus Christ and Him crucified. [3] I came to you in weakness with great fear and trembling. [4] My message and my preaching were not with wise and persuasive words, but with a demonstration of the Spirit's power, [5] so that your faith might not rest on human wisdom, but on God's power.
(1 Corinthians 2v1–5)

The Gospel declares that "Jesus is Lord" (Romans 10:9). This was dangerous talk in New Testament times, as it was a direct challenge to the Roman Empire who taught "Caesar is Lord". The Gospel is Trinitarian, in that it is the Father's mysterious revelation through the Son's work on the cross in the power of the Holy Spirit.

The Gospel is also Three Dimensional in that it covers the breadth of the Bible – all of Scripture is about God's plan of Salvation; the depth of the cross of Jesus Christ and the length of God's mission.
The Gospel was, and is, anathema and unpopular to those outside of the Kingdom of God.

In the New Testament, it was a direct challenge to the ancient Roman Empire. Today, this thinking is also here, particularly in those countries where Christianity is actively persecuted. The Gospel is never popular, and if it is, then it is not a truly Biblical Gospel.

For instance, some Churches proclaim a false Gospel where financial and health prosperity is the central claim. This is a false Gospel where Jesus is a cure-all being the central claim. There is also a false Gospel wherever it is used for political purposes. The true Gospel of the New Testament is "Jesus and Him crucified" (1 Corinthians 2:2).

The claim that "Jesus is Lord of all" was a direct and dangerous challenge to the prevailing idea throughout the Roman empire that Caesar was Lord of all. Jesus' exclusive claim to be the only way, the only truth and the only life challenges pluralism and universalism.

In the ancient world, as today, there are plenty of gods available, why would people settle for just the One true God. Particularly one who had died. A life of holiness, morality and right living challenges immorality.

God's power challenges cultured intellect who consider it as mere babbling. Humility challenges pride, for to kneel at the cross, takes great humility and this would have been derided and classed as utter blathering nonsense. Where people are proud and cultured, the very thought of humbly kneeling before a God is anathema.

We can be shouted down if we dare exclaim that Jesus is Lord and the only acceptable path to God. We are told in the media and by people, that Jesus Christ is not significant.

We are told that there are no such thing as moral absolutes anymore, that what's morally right for us, may not be right for others and we are stay out of others private

Sex and sexuality are worshipped and adored as if they were gods in themselves.

We live in an age of humanism, scientific materialism and hyper-rationalism, where people cynically laugh at Christians and say that we worship a dead man, if He even existed at all, and that we are fools for believing in a God. Humility is not looked upon as a strength today.

Humility is often frowned upon as a weakness. The prevalent worldview in the western communities, says that if we want to get ahead in life, we need to be strong, show some backbone, don't ever back down to anybody or anything and most certainly, never admit that we were wrong and have made mistakes.

The way of the Gospel, the way for the Christian, however, is for us to kneel before the Cross of Jesus Christ, admit our mistakes and sins and be prepared to serve and take up our own cross.

This is directly antagonistic to the prevailing worldview and culture of the western community. They are quite willing to accept a harmless baby at Christmas, but not the violence of the cross that followed at Easter.

Evangelism can only be truly effective when undertaken under an umbrella of prayer and the work of the Holy Spirit.

It is the Holy Spirit's power and authority, which allows the skills and talents of all people, to be used as effective Gospel messengers.

As Christians, we need to continually remind ourselves that it is Jesus Christ who is building the Church, and that with the Holy Spirit's power, we are neither alone nor powerless.

After all, He is the Holy Spirit of evangelism. That is why we need not fear the supposed rise of fundamental atheism, humanism, or any other religion or – "ism". We have the power of the living God within us, to equip and use us for His glory, honour and mission.

People may be able to remove the supposed 'spirit of Christmas' from schools and other government buildings, but they can never take away the Spirit of Christ that indwells us and all Christians.

The world around us, with the help of Satan, likes to play clever tricks on us.

But we are to be different, to be discerning and wise, as Jesus commanded His followers to "be as shrewd as snakes and as innocent as doves." (Matthew 10:16)

As Christians, we are to stay faithful to Jesus and that sometimes is difficult. It means staying faithful to Jesus and His will, regardless of any opposition and attractive alternatives which confront us.

By doing this we will endure and remain faithful to Him. In doing so we will be strengthened and energized for the work that Jesus Christ, our God, has set for us to do, as part of His Church, His body, here in the world, wherever we go and whatever we are doing.

The early Church preached that God, who is outside of both time and space, entered human time and history as a human baby. This baby was Jesus, and His purpose was to surrender His life as a ransom for many people (Mark 10:45). The early Church grew expansively.

What clues and tips can we take from them to help me? The Apostle Paul evangelised wherever people gathered together, such as at the Synagogue (Acts 18:4, 6) as well as in the marketplace or place of work (Acts 18:3, 13). Paul certainly had his fears, frustrations and limitations of his own weaknesses.

However, he overcame them and used these experiences as a means to rely totally on God's power and strength. The same is indeed true for us today if we are honest with ourselves.

If that is where Paul shared the message, what are some of the various methods that he employed, which can help us as we seek to be obedient to the command of Jesus Christ?

Paul knew that Scripture revealed God's programme and he was always prepared to change strategy (Acts 18:6). Paul was invited into homes of others (Acts 18:7) and he was careful to forge relationships (Acts 18:2, 7–8 & 17) with people.
Paul's Gospel message was "Jesus and Him crucified" (1 Corinthians 2:2).

The Gospel is Jesus and that is why it is so central to the Gospel message. As important as the incarnation, crucifixion, resurrection and ascension are, the Gospel is Jesus.

Not just a Jesus to whom anything can be attached, such as being a good friend.

But the real and historical Jesus who was God–man, lived in this world, was falsely accused, condemned, crucified, died, rose again and ascended into heaven.

In other words, the whole story of His life and death. At the very centre of that story, and most significant for us, was His death that secured our salvation and His resurrection which proved that He was the Messiah that He said He was.

⁶ This is the one who came by water and blood – Jesus Christ. He did not come by water only, but by water and blood. And it is the Spirit who testifies, because the Spirit is the truth. ⁷ For there are three that testify: ⁸ the Spirit, the water and the blood; and the three are in agreement. ⁹ We accept human testimony, but God's testimony is greater because it is the testimony of God, which He has given about His Son. ¹⁰ Whoever believes in the Son of God accepts this testimony. Whoever does not believe God has made Him out to be a liar, because they have not believed the testimony God has given about His Son. ¹¹ And this is the testimony: God has given us eternal life, and this life is in His Son. ¹² Whoever has the Son has life; whoever does not have the Son of God does not have life.

(1 John 5:9–12)

To all this, we tell our own story of how Jesus came into our lives and transformed us. One thing that all Christians have, is a testimony, which is a story of how that person became a follower of Jesus Christ.

A testimony is an assertion offering first-hand authentication of a fact. For us, as Christians, our testimony is initially about how we came to be Christians, expresses why we are Christians, and what that means to us now. So a testimony is not just how but also why.

Now, I could say that at as a teenager, I was invited along to a local youth group at the Baptist Church, and several weeks later, gave my life to Christ and became a Christian. That is, of course, partly true. The reason that I am a Christian is not because I chased God, but rather He chased me, following my every path with the urgency of a lover after the beloved.

We are Christians, not because we attend Church services, or we that we happened to have been born in a supposedly Christian country. We are Christians entirely because God first chased and harried us into His arms.

We are Christians, because God first loved us, and He beckoned and called us by name to respond to His call and follow Him.

We are Christians not because of anything we have done, but rather because He first chased us, and because He first loved us.

Jesus Himself said:
"For the Son of Man did not come to be served but to serve, and to give His life give His life as a ransom for many" (Mark 10:45).

We are Christians today, because of the joint events at Christmas and Easter when God entered this world as a human baby we know as Jesus Christ. He took all the necessary steps so that all people could have the choice to be His follower, His person, or not.

We read about the growth of the early church in the Book of Acts in the Bible. Christianity is a faith whereby all Christians, all followers of Jesus, are to tell others of the goodness of God.

As followers of Jesus Christ, all we are to evangelize. Evangelism is showing and telling others of God's message of reconciliation to all people of all time.

Evangelism is not, as some proclaim, of forcing people to adopt Church standards (1 Corinthians 5:12) and nor is it simply a message of join the church as a symbol of good works (Ephesians 2:8-10).

If people know you are a Christian, they will be watching how you behave, conduct yourself in your life and your words. You are a witness for God – whether you want to be or not. Let's be good witnesses.

The prime motivation for evangelism is out of gratitude for what God has done, in that we love Him because He loved us first.

We are all to do the work of an evangelist (2 Timothy 4:5) even though not everybody has the specific gift of being an evangelist. But we are not just to evangelise but also disciple. Intentionally make disciples of Jesus Christ.

In the last words of Matthew's Gospel, all Christian Disciples are to make disciples throughout the whole earth:

18 Then Jesus came to them and said, 'All authority in heaven and on earth has been given to me. 19 Therefore go and make disciples of all nations, baptising them in the name of the Father and of the Son and of the Holy Spirit, 20 and teaching them to obey everything I have commanded you. And surely I am with you always, to the very end of the age.' (Matthew 28:18-20).

God the Holy Spirit is living within us, which is a constant reminder to us that it is by grace alone through faith alone, that we are children of the Living God.

That is part of the message of Evangelism: people throughout the world, including the communities in which we live and work, can choose to become children of God.

# 4. Shield of Faith

22 Immediately Jesus made the disciples get into the boat and go on ahead of him to the other side, while he dismissed the crowd. 23 After he had dismissed them, he went up on a mountainside by himself to pray. Later that night, he was there alone, 24 and the boat was already a considerable distance from land, buffeted by the waves because the wind was against it.
25 Shortly before dawn Jesus went out to them, walking on the lake. 26 When the disciples saw him walking on the lake, they were terrified. 'It's a ghost,' they said, and cried out in fear.
27 But Jesus immediately said to them: 'Take courage! It is I. Don't be afraid.'
28 'Lord, if it's you,' Peter replied, 'tell me to come to you on the water.'
29 'Come,' he said. Then Peter got down out of the boat, walked on the water and came towards Jesus. 30 But when he saw the wind, he was afraid and, beginning to sink, cried out, 'Lord, save me!' 31 Immediately Jesus reached out his hand and caught him. 'You of little faith,' he said, 'why did you doubt?' 32 And when they climbed into the boat, the wind died down. 33 Then those who were in the boat worshipped him, saying, 'Truly you are the Son of God.'
(Matthew 14v22-33).

The common idea, indeed, prevalent in the western worldview, is that faith, or belief, is one step down from knowledge. People talk about making the 'leap of faith'. Things that we know and are self-evidential, are rock solid.

Whereas things that we 'merely' believe without any form of evidence are not solid but rather they are things we just hope are true and right, but we cannot be absolutely sure of them.

That may be true of some of the things we believe and have faith in, but it is certainly not true of Biblical faith.

The Christian faith is founded on one solid fact: the resurrection of Jesus Christ from the dead. This is one of the best-attested fact of ancient history. Yet many people feel they can doubt that it actually happened.

Everybody accepts that Julius Caesar was assassinated in 44BC, yet the evidence of that event is far thinner than the evidence for the resurrection of Jesus Christ.

Why the difference in attitude to the two events?

The answer to that question is that many leaders have been assassinated down through the years, but the resurrection of Jesus was a once only event.

Because the assassination was repeated it is accepted; because there has been only one resurrection, it is not acknowledged.
That argument is very understandable, but it is neither correct or right.

It was in the very nature of the event, the salvation moment for all humanity, that it could never be repeated. It had to be a once and for all moment.

But in order to prepare the people of that time, and everybody who has lived since, God carried out a series of events that teaches, step by step, that it was all completely possible.

In particular, the redemption of the people from Egypt, over a thousand years earlier, teaches about redemption.

The repeated sacrifices in the Jerusalem temple teaches about sacrifice.
The lives of people such as Moses and David demonstrate what the life of a true person of God would look like.

If the one event could not be repeated, it at least could be explained in advance and very carefully prepared for in great detail. It was not a completely strange event. Rather, it was only strange within its intensity, its force and its importance.

When we say that we have faith in the Lord Jesus or when we say we believe in the existence of God, we are therefore not operating on a lower level than when we say that we know the sun is behind the clouds even although we cannot see the sun.

Ergo, we are placing our confidence in an event that happened a long time ago, but we can do so because the event is welded solidly into human history over many years, centuries and millennia.
What is faith? People say that faith is blind.

The Bible, however, tells us that faith can be defined as a total confidence in God's faithfulness, which leads us in all aspects of life, to have complete reliance upon Him, trust in Him and show total obedience to Him (Hebrews 11:6).

We see this faith in the Godly obedience of those around us who know Him, as well as hearing the testimonies and stories of those from the Bible and from Church history.

To secure salvation, faith is a voluntary change of mind and heart in the sinner, whereby we turn to God, applying our own will to accepting God's offer of salvation through Jesus Christ, His Son. All parts of us are being transformed.

Firstly, there is our emotions or heart, and our personal assent to the gospel. We asked of ourselves, "What must we do to be saved?", whereby we agree to make salvation a prime part of our life.

Secondly, our will, which is a personal trust in Jesus Christ.

Lastly, our mind, in which we recognise our need of salvation and acknowledge Jesus Christ's death on our behalf and our need of forgiveness for those sins. As followers of Jesus, we are to continue having faith in Him.

There are four things at least, we are to have faith in Him for. By faith, Jesus Christ is praying for us. (Romans 8:34). He knew the troubles of the disciples (Mark 6:48), just as He knows our troubles now.

Jesus feels our cares and knowing what we are going through, He is encouraging us to continue to trust Him in all aspects of life because of His own experiences during His earthly life (Hebrews 4:14-16).

By faith, God Himself will come to us. After all, His Holy Spirit is living within us, sealing us as God's very child.

If we ever think that God has abandoned us, then we are not alone in thinking such things at times. King David often felt that God was far away and unconcerned about what He was undergoing (Psalm 22:1-21). However, King David also knew that God would ultimately rescue Him (Psalm 22:22-31).

Jesus always comes to us through difficult times, although He may not come in the time that we think He should come. We trust Jesus because He knows when we need Him most and will come then.

King David often felt God was far away and unconcerned. However he also knew God would ultimately rescue Him. Paul, the great Apostle, also felt himself to be under pressure (2 Corinthians 1:8)

By faith, Jesus will help us grow. One time the disciples were in boat on the stormy sea and Jesus came to them walking on the water (Matthew 14:25). The purpose of that incident was to show that they had to learn to trust in Him when He wasn't physically present since He would be soon leaving them.

Perhaps this is what Peter was thinking of when later on in His life, he quotes the Psalmist

"For the eyes of the Lord are on the righteous and His ears are attentive to their prayer, but the face of the Lord is against those who do evil." (1 Peter 3:12)

By faith, therefore, God will see us through all things. He has done so for us in the past and He will do so again in the future.

Jesus said to Peter, "Come" and Peter went to Jesus walking on the water (Matthew 14:29). This must have encouraged the other disciples, for when they saw Jesus' power, they worshipped Him. Whatever troubles we are undergoing are temporary, and Jesus will see us through. By faith in Christ, we have salvation.

By faith Jesus is praying for us, will come to us, grow us and help us through our concerns, worries and troubles, regardless of what they may be.

By being obedient to God, we are showing our salvation to other people.

We are showing that faith is not blind and inert as some propose, but rather we display that faith is dynamic and active.

By being obedient to God, we are showing our salvation to other people. We are showing that faith is not blind and inert as some propose, but rather we display that faith is dynamic and active.

Through, and by faith in Jesus Christ alone, as Christians, we persevere. This is the perseverance in relation to God and His work, which is the continuous operation of the Holy Spirit in our life as Christian believers.

It is a work of divine grace that is begun in our heart when we became Christians, and which will be continued with and brought to completion.

Because of God's perseverance and His complete and utter reliability, our faith and we will never perish, and nobody can snatch us out of His hand (John 10:27-29). The good work that God began in us, will be carried on to completion (Philippians 1:6), as we are shielded by God's almighty power (1 Peter 1:5).

We hold onto the fact that nobody or nothing can separate us from the love of God that is in Christ Jesus, our Lord (Romans 8:38-39). We persevere in faith, based on the fact that Jesus Christ knows those who are His people (2 Timothy 2:19).

Our eternal life never depends on our own feeble grip on Jesus Christ, but rather on His firm grip upon us, as we are fulfilling God's purpose of transforming us into the very image of His Son, Jesus.

This is where perseverance for us as Christians comes in. Through faith, we persevere by keeping our eyes focussed on Jesus Christ throughout each day and being obedient to Him. As followers of Jesus, we persevere in faith with

This is evidenced as we obey Him and follow Him closely, asking Him questions humbly and expecting Him to answer. Particularly if we don't understand something. By faith, God will persevere with us, turning us gradually into the image of His Son, Jesus Christ.

We hold firmly, in His strength, to the shield of faith.

# 5. Helmet of Salvation

"My dear friends, as you have always obeyed—not only in my presence, but now much more in my absence—continue to work out your salvation with fear and trembling, for it is God who works in you to will and to act in order to fulfil His good purpose." (Philippians 2v12-13)

Salvation means 'a rescue' or 'having been saved'. As humans, when we were born, we inherited that sinful nature we looked at earlier and were subsequently alienated from God.

But God has seen fit to offer a way back into relationship with Him, so that we may no longer be alienated from Him.

This offer of relationship is a result of Jesus, who was both fully God and fully human, dying on the cross at Calvary.

We are saved because this is an act of salvation, which is available for all people of all time and of every nation. As Christians, we have accepted the offer and we are to live so as to please God alone as a priority above our own self or of that of anybody else.

The question "Who decides the saved?" has been asked for centuries. There are two extremist views – one view states "God has decided all things, and nothing can be done about it." The other view is, "universalism", which states that God will grant salvation to all, regardless of creed, race or religion.

But we need to see these two views in the balance of Scripture. Firstly, God does choose individuals to fulfil His purposes (Romans 9) and He chooses those who are, or will be, saved (John 15:16). These chosen ones are called the elect.

However, it is also equally true, that it is His will that all people should be saved (1 Timothy 2:3-4) and that nobody should perish (2 Peter 3:9).

Therefore, we must accept that both these Scriptural statements are equally and absolutely true. When we use words concerning God that have a time element attached, such as 'chose' or 'elect', we need to consider God's infinite time framework and His timelessness.

God does not work in our human finite time framework. As Christians, we are now saved from everlasting alienation from Him, for that is what hell is.

Instead, we are saved into an everlasting relationship with Him, for that is what heaven is.

One day, as Christians, we will die and be with Jesus, who is our Lord, our King, our Saviour and our friend. We will be with for eternity in a place we know as heaven.

What is this place of heaven like? People, both believers and non-believers have an opinion about heaven. To many people, heaven is where everybody will meet up after death, providing that they were not too bad in this earthly life.

The caricature of comedians is that in heaven, everybody not exceedingly bad, will be floating around on clouds and playing a harp.

What does the Bible, have to say about heaven?

The first thing to say is that heaven is a physical place with the physical properties as a house (John 14:2), a Kingdom (Matthew 25:34), paradise (2 Corinthians 12:2-4) and a Holy City (Revelation 21:2).

Heaven is part of the inheritance of all Christians. (1 Peter 1:4). Heaven is a place replete with glory (Romans 8:17–18), joy (Luke 15:7–10), peace (Luke 16:19–25), reward (Matthew 5:11–12), rest (Revelation 14:13), righteousness (2 Peter 3:13) and service (Revelation 7:15). No sitting around on clouds there! For instance, service implies working.

Who is heaven prepared for and who can enter? Heaven is for all those recorded in the Book of Life (Malachi 3:16–18, Philippians 4:3; Revelation 20:12).
As we have salvation and that God has declared us to be righteous (Matthew 5:20), and holy (Revelation 19:8), we will be seen amongst the obedient (Revelation 22:14).

We will enter heaven through giant gates of pearl (Revelation 21:21). A pearl is formed as an oyster suffers, covering a grain of irritating sand, until the irritation ceases.

Now what do you think the suffering was, that created these giant pearls that are the gates? It can only be the cross of Jesus Christ and the incredible suffering and pain that He endured upon it.

Only through the pain, the agony and the suffering that Jesus endured, culminating in His death as He cried out:
"My God! Our God! Why have you forsaken me?" (Matthew 27:46).

It is only through the death of Jesus on the cross that we can be declared holy and righteous.

Only those who have been declared as such will be able to be in the presence of Almighty God. Those who have been declared holy, are only those who have embraced Jesus Christ during their earthly life and followed

As Christians, our current attitude towards heaven should be to desire it (2 Corinthians 5:2–8), eagerly keep watch for it (2 Peter 3:13) and to put our treasure there (Luke 12:32–34).
God the Son, Jesus Christ, has prepared a place for all those who love Him, trust Him and obey Him as King.

¹ Then I saw 'a new heaven and a new earth,' for the first heaven and the first earth had passed away, and there was no longer any sea. ² I saw the Holy City, the new Jerusalem, coming down out of heaven from God, prepared as a bride beautifully dressed for her husband. ³ And I heard a loud voice from the throne saying, 'Look! God's dwelling-place is now among the people, and He will dwell with them. They will be His people, and God Himself will be with them and be their God. ⁴ "He will wipe every tear from their eyes. There will be no more death" or mourning or crying or pain, for the old order of things has passed away.' (Revelation 21:1–4)

From this picture given by John, Heaven is also a pure place. In this earthly life, every human suffers in some way. We know that we have in the past, we do currently and will in the future. When our King returns, man's inhumanity to man will no longer be allowed.

One day, there will be no more pain, death, suffering and sin. Perfection will be reached, and it is to the glory of an Almighty and merciful God, that this will occur.

Two words of gentle warning though.

Firstly, all that, is describing the indescribable, in human terms. For the simple reason there is no other way to do it.

So, therefore, we need to be careful at how literally we take it.

Secondly, it seems that it is not heaven that is our destination, but the new heavens and the new, that is revived, earth (Romans 8:22-25; Revelation 21:1).

How those two interlock is not at all clear and, it quite possibly serves as a deliberate reminder that we should be cautious as we look down the tunnel of time to the light at the far end.

At Christmas, we celebrate Jesus Christ coming to earth as a human. Christmas is a time where the Church and our community celebrate Jesus Christ's first coming as a baby.

The community like to think of Jesus as a baby, because a baby can be controlled, to a degree. Society in general, is comfortable with leaving Jesus as a baby.

However, Jesus is not a baby now. Jesus is King and what a King. He has promised that He is coming again, not as a baby, but as King and judge.
When we Christians get to heaven, Jesus has prepared a place for all who love Him, trust Him and obey Him as King.

Our King is waiting for us! He is expecting us, wanting to lavish His love upon us.
We know He loves us now, but this is only in part.

When we are with Him eternally, we shall have the full picture of Jesus. He is with us now in Spirit, but then we shall be with Him physically and face to face.

Heaven is a prepared place of majestic beauty.

One glorious day, all suffering will be banished for those who love Jesus now and He will wipe the tears from our eyes, as He takes our face in His hands (Revelation 21:4).

What a glorious day it will be for those who like us, love God now.

God Himself, with our face in His hands, wiping away our tears. It will be a place where we will live the fruit of the spirit eternally.

It will be an amazing place where the fruit of the Spirit, "love, joy, peace, longsuffering, kindness, goodness, faithfulness, gentleness and self-control" (Galatians 5:22-23) are both permanent and universal.

This is all part of the manifesto of Jesus, our King. What a wondrous and glorious day that will be! We will enter those gates, thanking Jesus. We will be able to say with other Christian believers, "It was worth it all."

Heaven is prepared for us, and it is a pure place. Our King Himself has suffered for us, so that we may enjoy His company forever and ever, if we only trust and obey Him now and place our faith in Him while we are here in this our temporal home on earth. We know in part now, but then we will know in full.

This makes the sins that we commit while we are here on earth as we follow Jesus, even more serious. Sometimes we take a rather blasé attitude to sin. We excuse them as only a minor thing and of no real consequence.

Each time we sin as a believer, it is as if we are spitting in the very face of Jesus. Our desire should be, to be Jesus and to be like Him. We long to be perfect. When we make a mistake and sin, we cry out in frustration to be perfect now!

However, we also know that God is smoothing our rough edges to continue making us purer, more like His Son and our King, under the power and direction of the Holy Spirit.

We can only enter heaven, our new home, through the cross of Jesus Christ. When we first decided for Jesus and turned over our lives to Him, that is when our eternal life with Him commenced. Heaven is our home and one day we will be with our King forever.

In the meantime, when we sin, we are to keep a short account and ask for forgiveness as soon as we recognise that we have sinned, and the Holy Spirit has convicted us of it. We yearn to be with our King for ever and ever.

Yet, we are to keep one part of our mind on Heaven and the other on the responsible work we have been set to do, here on earth.

We are not to be so heavenly minded, that we are of no earthly use. We are also not to be so earth bound, that we are not tied to King Jesus in our eternal home.

We are to go and tell others about Jesus. Heaven is a great big place, and there will be room for everybody to enter through one of those twelve gates!

Jesus Christ is our King of Righteousness. We are to fully trust Him and live a life worthy of Him, while looking for His coming back again!

We are to be expectant, for our King is coming back for us soon! He has promised and He will do it!

Jesus is completely and utter dependable, reliable and worthy of our trust in Him. Our God, our King Jesus, will appear soon. He is coming back as the King of Righteousness, in order to judge evil and reject those who reject Him whilst rewarding those who patiently trust and obey Him.

The great enemy, Satan, is defeated, he is beaten, and he will no longer be any threat (Revelation 12:7-10). Same with other adversaries, our old nature and sin. All defeated. because of Jesus Christ, the Son of God.

As we are engaged in battle, we persevere in the power of the Holy Spirit. In His strength, we overcome all adversaries, knowing that Jesus is King, that we are His, He has called us by name to follow Him and He is coming back for us because He loves us.

We can echo the words of the Apostle John, whom Jesus loved: "Come, Lord Jesus!" (Revelation 22:20).
We can only praise God for this and await that day. Knowing that we have been saved by God alone. We are saved by and through God alone and we will be saved due to God alone, from His wellsprings of grace and mercy.

We have been, are, and will be saved to a life living with God. All because of Jesus Christ. To follow Jesus Christ is to participate in salvation. We are saved. We are being saved. We will be saved. The three great tenses of salvation.
We wear the helmet of salvation.

# 6. Sword of the Spirit

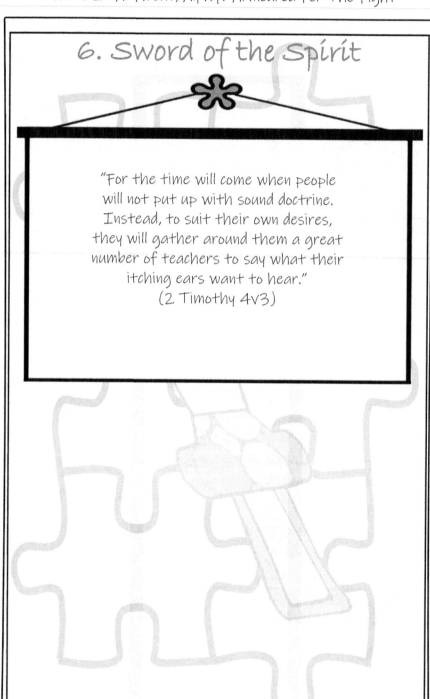

"For the time will come when people will not put up with sound doctrine. Instead, to suit their own desires, they will gather around them a great number of teachers to say what their itching ears want to hear."
(2 Timothy 4v3)

Another weapon of spiritual warfare is the sword of the Spirit. This is God's Word, the Bible, which is the primary way by which we hear God speak.
Throughout the Bible God is revealed, whereby He makes Himself known to all sorts of people from all kinds of backgrounds.

People are not naturally born possessing this knowledge, even though they know God's very existence. Acknowledging that God exists is different from actually knowing God personally.

Personal knowledge of God is ultimately crucial however, since knowing God personally and developing the relationship is what being a Christian is all about.

As Christians, we should be rejoicing that God earnestly desires us to attain this knowledge of Him, in order to know Him more and more.

For this reason, He has spoken to us through His Word, the Bible, revealing Himself and disclosing how we may know Him more.

Whilst God can be known, our knowledge of God is partial, and we will never know everything there is to be known about Him. Knowledge of Him is both wondrous and without end.

As we grow spiritually, knowing the Bible and thus knowing Him more, we will grow in spiritual maturity.

The Apostle Peter commands that we grow in the knowledge of Jesus (2 Peter 3:18). We do this as part of our spiritual journey in order to become more like Jesus.

One of the Christian life's' greatest delights, is developing an intimate knowledge of God and relationship with Him. The gospel, or the good news of Jesus Christ, which we share with others, is entitled 'the power of God to salvation'.

The Bible, and its gospel by which people come to know God, is the agent of the new birth.

It is the soap or cleansing agent whereby God gives the believing sinner a spiritual bath resulting in salvation.

The Bible is a teacher that brings wisdom which leads to salvation.

As Christians, we believe that God has spoken to this world because He loves this world. The Apostle John tells us that God is love (1 John 4:16).

An inherent part of love is a desire to both know and to be known.

One aspect of that love is the reason as to why God became man in Jesus Christ, because God wanted to know and be known in the fullest, human way possible.

Another aspect of God's love is the reason the prophets spoke, history was recorded, and the Bible was therefore written. God wanted His message to be given to all people.

But what are Christians to believe about the Bible?

There are three words which summarize what Christians are to believe about the Bible.

It is God's revealed word about His Son Jesus Christ, which is inspired by His Holy Spirit and illuminated within us as we seek Him.

One of the Christian life's' greatest delights, is developing an intimate knowledge of God and relationship with Him. The gospel, or the good news of Jesus Christ, which we share with others, is entitled 'the power of God to salvation'.

What do we mean when we say God has spoken to the world using those three methods through the Bible? Revelation, whereby God has caused the truth to be revealed. Inspiration since God has caused the truth to be recorded. Finally, Illumination where God causes the truth to be understood.

The Bible, as God's written word, is revelation. Revelation is how God has communicated truths to people, who otherwise would not know them.

The story of creation in Genesis 1 and 2 is a good example of this.

As humanity was not created until the sixth day, it must have been God who revealed the knowledge about what occurred on the first five days to the author of Genesis, or it would not be possible to know what occurred.

We know God spoke to those who wrote the Bible, but how did He speak? We know that He spoke to them in their own language, just as He did to young Samuel in the temple. Samuel at first thought that the voice was that of Eli the priest (1 Samuel 3:3–9).

At other times God spoke through angels, such as when the angel Gabriel informed Mary that she would give birth to Jesus (Luke 1:26–38).

In the Old Testament, God often spoke through the "Angel of the Lord" (Judges 2:4; Zechariah 1:12). Some people believe this to have been Jesus before He came to earth as a human (Joshua 5:13–15; 1 Chronicles 21:16). These events are called a 'christophany', which is a pre-incarnate appearance of Jesus the Son of God.

God also communicated in dreams and visions. An example of this is in the birth story of Jesus Christ, where the wise men were warned in a dream not to return to King Herod (Matthew 2:12). God has also communicated from a burning bush (Exodus 3) and from within a cloud (Exodus 34).

God has even spoken through a donkey, as the prophet Balaam can testify (Numbers 22). Without revelation, we could not learn about God.

Unless God reveals Himself, we would not know anything about Him.

We know for certain that this revelation has caused the Bible, the Written Word of God, to reveal Jesus Christ, the Living Word of God.

As Christians, we also believe the Bible is inspired. But what do we mean by that? The actual word 'inspiration' is found only once in the New Testament, when Paul explicitly states:
"All Scripture is given by inspiration of God" or more literally "All Scripture is God-breathed" (2 Timothy 3:16).

The word 'inspiration' is actually not the best translation. The original Greek word says God 'breathed out' His Word. Divine inspiration naturally proceeds from divine revelation.

While through revelation God speaks to humanity, it is by inspiration that God works the pen, ergo ensuring that the message is God breathed and written correctly. This process of inspiration has a number of theories attached to it.

One theory called the content theory, suggests that the author was given the main idea by God, but God allowed the writer to choose their own words. Another is the natural theory. This is where the Biblical writers were inspired in the same sense Shakespeare was inspired, but that doesn't agree with the 'God-breathed' word.

It is quite apparent that God did not suppress the writers' personalities.

For example, the writing style of John is clearly different from that of Peter or indeed that of Paul.

The differences in writing style and in vocabulary of different authors are easily seen.

However, Jesus implied clearly that God chose the very letters of the words when He said that not one stroke of the pen would pass from the law (Matthew 5:17–19). From this, we can infer that God inspires all the words of the Bible. God wanted to communicate to ordinary people, therefore He used ordinary people to write and produce the Bible.

In response to temptation by Satan, Jesus said that humanity is to live by God's inspired words (Matthew 4:4, 7 & 10).

Writers in the Bible, such as Peter, knew their writings were being guided by God (1 Peter 1:10–12; 2 Peter 1:19–20, 3:15–16).

Inspiration is only guaranteed in the original manuscripts which were written in Hebrew, Greek or Aramaic.

It is not, however much some people protest, guaranteed in any translation of the Bible.

God has spoken and He has communicated His written word to humanity. Firstly, by revelation when God spoke to the writers. Secondly, through inspiration, as God divinely guided the writers, in the process of writing His message.

However, in order to understand God's revealed and inspired message, illumination is required.

This is where God causes the Bible to be understood by both the human heart and the mind. Without illumination, we continue to be blinded by our own old nature and by Satan.

Just as a light bulb needs power in order to give light, so the Bible needs somebody to provide the power. The person, who does this illuminating, is God the Holy Spirit.

Jesus promised that the Holy Spirit would illuminate the Bible to the hearts and minds of all those people willing to listen, both Christian and non-Christian.

Take for example the event recorded in Acts 2. This is where the Holy Spirit uses God's Word to illuminate sinners at Pentecost, where after hearing Peter preach, over three thousand people became Christians (Acts 2:41).

As Christians, we also need this illumination to help us to understand the Bible. The Holy Spirit will reveal truths to us as we read the Bible regularly, asking for His help in understanding it.

God's Living Word Jesus Christ is revealed as the Holy Spirit illuminates the Bible as God's inspired written word. That way people's lives are transformed and changed.

Therefore, we continue to pray for His help and illumination when reading the Bible, God's written Word.

We hold fast the sword of the Spirit, which is the Bible, God's written Word which reveals God's Living Word, Jesus Christ.

# About The Author

I was born in a small country town in Australia. I was raised to be a sceptical agnostic/atheist with the words "Churches are dangerous places" ringing in my ears. Coming into my teenage years, I decided if Churches are so dangerous, let's rebel and go for a bit of danger. So I rebelled, became a Christian, started attending a local Christian youth group and was baptized.

In 1990, I came to the UK for 6 months' travel around Europe. Or so I thought. I have stayed ever since. I view it as God having a sense of humour. He knows I don't like rain, cold and in particular – together. He has even given me the most beautiful of women as a wife, but she doesn't like hot weather. God sure has a sense of humour.

In 2003, I had a stroke and I took redundancy from my job. I went off to Moorlands College where I graduated in 2007. Later that year, I set up Partakers Ministries.

I currently reside with my wife in Bournemouth in the UK. I travel often to speak in places including the USA and Australia and would love to see you. I hope you have enjoyed this book and perhaps learnt something afresh or as a reminder. Please do contact me if I need clarification or disagree with something that is written here.

Peace and blessings.

# Other Books in the "What's It All About, Alphy?" Series

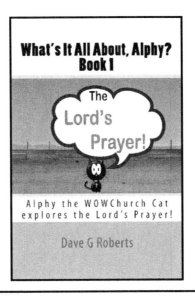

Have you ever been surprised by Grace? Grace is one of the wellsprings of God. Grace is a part of God's very nature! Now that may or may not be a surprise to you but that is only the beginning!

People who are in relationship with God are abundantly blessed by God! Can you believe that? Amazing, isn't it? In Romans 5, Paul gives 8 different glimpses, from different angles, about the surprise of grace for the Christian believer.

Paul is creating a fabulous spherical stained-glass window depicting life for the Christian believer who is now under grace and has Jesus as their Lord and master. Grace is a part of my story, just as it is for all Christian believers.

What surprises are in store for you, as you look into the amazing riches of the grace of God?

Books written to help you. Clearly.
www.pulptheology.com
www.pulptheology.co.uk

Come on in and explore with Alphy the WOWChurch Cat, what Paul has to say about the blessings and consequences of God's amazing grace.

Davo Roberts

## The Surprise of Grace

*Exploring Romans 5*

Have you ever been surprised by Grace?

Grace is not only amazing, but it is also surprising! Come inside with me, Alphy the WOWChurch Cat, and we will explore Romans 5:1-11 together and discover what it means for somebody to live under the grace of God. Are you ready?

We live in a troubled world. I wonder what challenges & tests you are undergoing currently in your life. Challenges of trouble and suffering come to us all in one way or another. As Christians, what are we to think of such challenges and troubles? The Bible as ever has much to say and to help guide us concerning this.

It has been said that in the Bible, all roads and paths ultimately lead to the book of Romans, in Romans 5 to 8, the Apostle Paul gives glimpses from different angles, of how the Christian should live under, and within, grace. Grace which is defined as God's unmerited favour to undeserving sinners. It's as if Paul is creating a fabulous stained glass sphere depicting life for the Christian believer. The Christian believer who is now under grace and has Jesus as their master and Lord.

Here in Romans 8, we come to another angle, with another scenario. Romans 8 is a passage of the Bible which is a fabulous jewel made of the purest of gold and the clearest of diamonds. Some people consider that interacting about this passage is akin to somebody trying to describe Beethoven's 9th Symphony with mere words. If that were true, then here in Romans 8, we have the Ode to Joy.

The challenges we face, of varying degrees, are common to all people of all time and of all cultures. Whether self-inflicted or inflicted by others, the challenges of troubles and sufferings unite all of humanity. It is a common denominator. Of course, there are no easy answers.

Come and join Alphy the WOWChurch Cat exploring this beautiful writing in Romans 8 and how it speaks to you as a Christian today, particularly as we deal with the daily challenges each of us face.

(Available in full colour on Kindle)

PULP theology
Books written to help you. Clearly.
www.pulptheology.com
www.pulptheology.co.uk

The Christian in Days of Challenge

Davo Roberts

G'day! I am Alphy the WOWChurch Cat! I am sure you know that we live in a troubled world, and our lives are full of challenges.

How are Christians to respond to those challenges? In Romans 8, a majestic piece of the Bible, we can discover a response to those challenges. Come on in!

Davo Roberts

# The Christian in Days of Challenge

What's It All About Alphy?
Alphy Looks Into Romans 8

---

"God, the Almighty One, has done great things for me, in giving me this Child", cries Mary. "As a virgin, there is no other way I could be with Child apart from God being involved. Praise be to His name - His name which is holy. My God is holy! That is who He is - the Almighty God of holiness."

"In order properly to understand this sacred hymn of praise, we need to bear in mind that the most blessed Virgin Mary is speaking out of her own experience, in which she was enlightened and instructed by the Holy Spirit." Martin Luther

"Now follows a remarkable and interesting song of the holy virgin, which plainly shows how eminent were her attainments in the grace of the Spirit." John Calvin

Mary's Song: The Magnificat

What's It All About, Alphy?

Davo Roberts

# Other Pulp Theology Books

AGOG: A Glimpse of God
An Ambassador in God's Orchestra of Joy
Dear Christian – Get A Good Grip
Dear Church: Wake up!
Developing Intimacy With God: A Little Book of 95 Prayers
Easter Essentials: Exploring Easter
Engaged In Battle
Exploring The Bible
God Gets His Hands Dirty
God, Internet Church & You
God's Two Words For You : Jesus and the Bible.
Helping the Forgotten Church
Heroes And Heretics Abound – History of the Church
Intimacy with God: The Christian Devotional Life
Living Life Right: Studies in Romans 12
Scriptural Delights: Exploring Psalm 119
The Surprise of Grace: Romans 5
When Love Hits Town
WOW Words of the Bible

## Glimpses Into Series:

Leviticus: A Book Of Joy
1 & 2 Chronicles: Books of heritage And history
Psalms: A Book Of Life
Ezekiel: A Book Of Symbols And Visions.
The Gospels: Books Of Good News
Acts: A Book Of Action
Romans: A Book Of Freedom

Volume 1: God Of The Bible
Volume 2: Jesus Christ
Volume 3: Being A Christian
Volume 4: The Church
Volume 5: Evangelism
Volume 6: The Christian Devotional Life

All books are available in Paperback and Kindle at:
PulpTheology.co.uk
PulpTheology.com


And all Amazon sites

# About Partakers

**Vision Statement:** Partakers exists to communicate and disseminate resources for the purposes of Christian Discipleship, Evangelism and Worship by employing radical and relevant methods, including virtual reality and online distribution.

**Mission Statement:** To help the world, one person at a time, to engage in whole life discipleship, as Partakers of Jesus Christ.

**Contact us to see how we can help you.** Seminars, coaching, preaching, teaching, discipleship or evangelism – offline or online.

**Email:** dave@partakers.co.uk
**Mobile:** 0794 794 5511
**Website:** http://www.partakers.co.uk